CONTENTS

WELCOME TO CHINA

Over a billion people live in China, the third-largest country in the world. China has many different regions, from snowy mountains and hot, sandy deserts, to rocky plains and sub-tropical forests. Most of China is still made up of vast, rural areas. But there are many big cities in China, and these are growing quickly.

▼ Many Chinese people work in farming. This woman in Guangxi Province waters her crops by hand.

C U [L T U R A L   J O U R N] E Y S

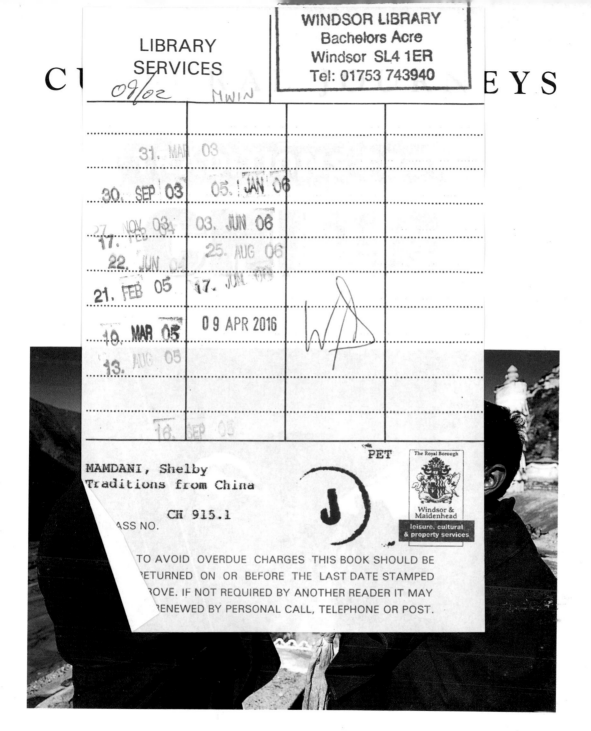

Shelby Mamdani

HODDER
Wayland

an imprint of Hodder Children's Books

CULTURAL JOURNEYS

Ni Hao. (A Mandarin greeting.)

TRADITIONS FROM
AFRICA

TRADITIONS FROM THE
CARIBBEAN

TRADITIONS FROM
CHINA

TRADITIONS FROM
INDIA

Cover: A young man plays pipes in Guangzhou. The border shows a tiled wall with a dragon motif.

Title page: Two Buddhist monks call other monks to prayer, using special conch shells. These shells represent the voice of Buddha.

Contents page: This little girl is wearing red, which the Chinese believe is a lucky colour.

Index: Two young Tibetan monks relax after a game of football.

Series editor: Katie Orchard
Designer: Tim Mayer
Production controller: Carol Stevens

First published in Great Britain in 1998 by Wayland Publishers Limited
This paperback edition published in 2002 by Hodder Wayland, an imprint of Hodder Children's Books

© Hodder Wayland 1998

Hodder Children's Books, a division of Hodder Headline Limited
338 Euston Road, London NW1 3BH

Picture Acknowledgements:
Axiom 32 (Jim Holmes), 48 (Gordon Clements); CEPHAS 17 (Nigel Blythe); Bruce Coleman Limited 6 (Hans Reinhard), 10 (Dr Stephen Coyne), 12 (Hans Reinhard); James Davis Travel Photography 21, 23, 28; Eye Ubiquitous *title page* (Bennett Dean), 19 (John Dakers), 29 (Julia Waterlow), 31 (Julia Waterlow), 41 (Julia Waterlow); Getty Images *contents page* (Keren Su), 4–5 (Andrew Errington), 8 (Alain le Garsmeur), 9 (Yann Layma), 14 (James Strachan), 18 (Anthony Cassidy), 26 (Glen Allison), 40 (Yann Layma); Robert Harding 20 (Yann Layma); Hutchison Library 15 (Trevor Page), 16 (Sarah Errington), 22 (Felix Greene), 37 (Sarah Murray); Images Photo Library *cover border*; Impact Photos 24 (Mark Henley), 35 (Christophe Bluntzer); Panos Pictures 11 (Sandrine Rousseau), 13 (Sandrine Rousseau), 27, 30 (Catherine Platt); Trip *main cover photo* (Eric Smith), 25 (Eric Smith), 38 (K. Cardwell); Wayland Picture Library 7, 33, 34, 36, 39, 42. The map illustration on page 4 is by Peter Bull. All border artwork for the interest boxes is by Pip Adams. The line illustrations for the story are by Helen Holroyd.

British Library Cataloguing in Publication Data
Mamdani, Shelby
Traditions from China.–(Cultural journeys)
1. China – Social life and customs – Juvenile literature
I. Title
390'.0951

ISBN 0 7502 4248 5

Typeset by Mayer Media
Printed and bound in Hong Kong.

Chinese people represent many different cultures. About 6 per cent of the people in China are non-Chinese ethnic minorities. Most of these minority groups live in five regions – Tibet, Inner Mongolia, Xinjiang, Ningxia and Guangxi.

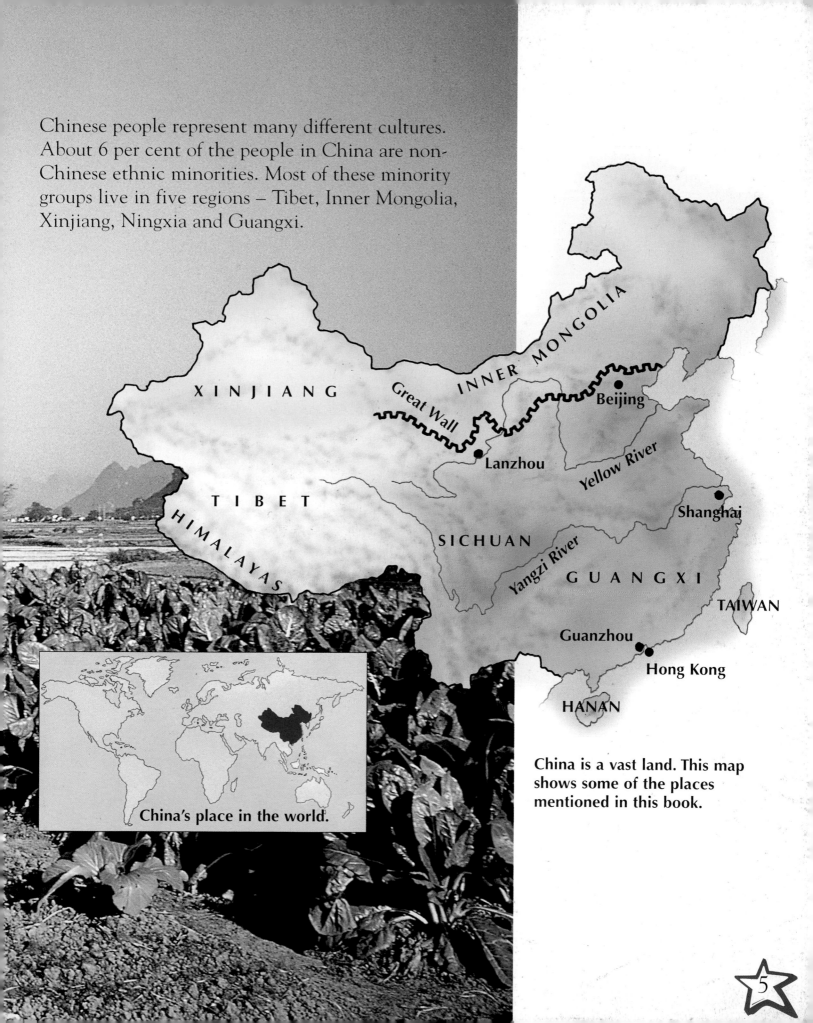

China's place in the world.

China is a vast land. This map shows some of the places mentioned in this book.

XINJIANG

INNER MONGOLIA

Great Wall

Beijing

Lanzhou

Yellow River

TIBET

HIMALAYAS

SICHUAN

Shanghai

Yangzi River

GUANGXI

TAIWAN

Guanzhou

Hong Kong

HANAN

The Written Language

A unique written language and a long history have united China for nearly 3,000 years. Chinese writing uses symbols called characters. Each character represents words, not sounds. Groups of people living in the different areas of China each spoke their own language. But they have always been able to communicate with people from other areas through the written language.

▼ **This girl is learning to write the characters for 'water' and 'field'. Together, these characters mean 'paddy field'.**

A Flourishing Trade

Since 1200 BC, the Chinese have traded ideas and goods with peoples around them. Trade and travel have helped to spread Chinese inventions and knowledge to Central Asia, the Middle East, and finally Europe and the rest of the world. Many people have left China for other parts of Asia, Europe, and North and South America. Most of these people came from the south-east coast of China, where sea trade to far-away places flourished from the very earliest times. Today, people with a Chinese background live all over the world. Their traditions have travelled with them.

▼ **These farmers are using horse power to plough their field.**

CHINESE FOOD

Food is an important part of Chinese culture. The Chinese have always eaten and enjoyed many different kinds of food from all over the country. Roasted or fried foods, such as duck, are famous in the north. In Guangzhou, in the east, light flavours and steamed food, such as *dim sum* dumplings are popular, while hot and spicy foods are a speciality in the western Sichuan region. In the south, Cantonese dishes feature plenty of seafood.

Chinese families believe that every kind of food has a 'warming' or 'cooling' quality. It is important to eat a correct balance of warm and cool foods to stay healthy.

▼ **This cook in Xinjiang Province is making some soup on an outdoor stove.**

Fast Food

Chinese food takes a lot of preparation, but it cooks quickly. One familiar style of cooking is 'stir-fry', in which several different foods are cooked in a special pan called a wok over a very high heat. Vegetables, noodles, meats or fish are often cooked in this way.

Many families living outside China today know about stir-fry cooking, and have a wok at home. Chinese food is now very popular with families all over the world.

▲ **Chopsticks have been used to eat food in China for over 3,000 years. This girl is just learning how to use them.**

Food Traditions

Food also plays an important part in traditional religious and family ceremonies in China. Over 3,000 years ago, people offered food to the spirits of their ancestors as part of special ceremonies. Food offerings were part of the responsibility of the living to care for the dead. In return, the ancestors would bring their living relatives good luck. Today, Chinese families still offer food to the spirits of dead family members on special days of the year.

▲ Chinese cooking uses a lot of spices for flavour. This stall in an indoor market sells all kinds of spices.

On special occasions, formal banquets or dinners are important parts of Chinese life. At these banquets, the host always serves food to guests sitting on either side of him or her. The guest of honour always sits to the right of the host and is served first. Then all the other guests are served. Banquets have many different courses. Some foods are believed to bring good luck. Noodles are often given at people's birthdays as they represent long life.

At informal family meals in restaurants, the food is placed in the centre of the table on a revolving tray. All the food is put on the table at once. This way everyone can reach whatever type of food takes their fancy.

▼ **This family has several different dishes to choose from. Everyone can choose some 'warming' and 'cooling' foods to make a balanced meal.**

Growing Tea

▼ This woman is hard at work, picking tea by hand.

Tea grows in the highland areas of southern China. Many people work picking the leaves and preparing them. Then the leaves are sorted and dried before they are packed for shipping to shops all over the world.

The custom of drinking tea first began in China over 2,000 years ago. At this time, monks drank tea to stay awake during long hours of meditation and prayer. Tea was so precious that it was used only in private societies, where members followed special rules for preparing and drinking it. Later, everyone could drink tea, and it became popular to offer it to visitors.

▲ **Friends still meet up to have a relaxing cup of tea and a chat.**

Tea was one of the main reasons why Europeans first journeyed to China. The tea plant could not survive in the cold European climates. So, explorers and traders travelled great distances to bring back enough tea to the cities of Europe to satisfy the huge demand. Traders brought back all kinds of cups and pots as well as tea. The word for fine porcelain, 'china,' is borrowed from the name for the country.

▲ This noodle-maker has put plenty of flour on the table to make sure the noodles don't stick together.

From China, noodles and dumplings have gradually made their way into Western cooking. Now people all over the world enjoy these foods. As people have moved from place to place, the technique of wrapping vegetables or meat in pastry has spread from China to many parts of the world. Some scholars believe that the famous fourteenth-century traveller Marco Polo introduced noodles and dumplings to Italy from China, 'inventing' spaghetti and ravioli.

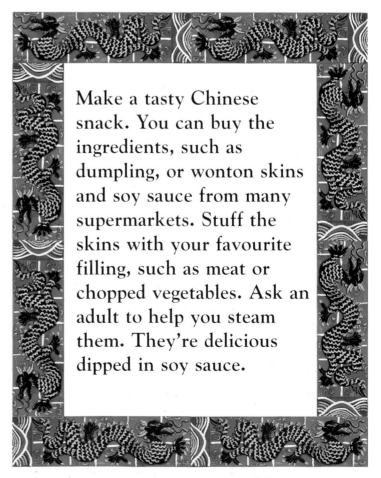

Make a tasty Chinese snack. You can buy the ingredients, such as dumpling, or wonton skins and soy sauce from many supermarkets. Stuff the skins with your favourite filling, such as meat or chopped vegetables. Ask an adult to help you steam them. They're delicious dipped in soy sauce.

Regional Foods

People in different parts of China eat food that is available locally. Rice is an important Chinese food, but it is grown only in the warm regions of the south. There, dishes with sweet and sour sauces, as well as lots of fish, are usually eaten with rice. Shark's fin soup is also a popular speciality of the area.

In western border areas, spicy or lemony dishes flavoured with hot peppers are common. In the eastern Yangtze River delta area, the heartland of China, people eat lots of fish and vegetables, such as bamboo shoots. They also cook with sweet and sour sauces.

In the north, wheat, millet and corn are more important staple foods. Northern dishes often include noodles, dumplings, breads and roasted meats, such as duck and pork.

▼ At this speciality food stall in Beijing, deep-fried scorpions are on the menu.

CLOTHES AND COSTUME

Many people in China today, especially in cities, wear Western-style clothing, but there are people in rural areas who still wear more traditional dress. Traditional summer clothing is made from cotton, linen or silk. During the winter months, some people wear quilted silk or cotton.

Silk

China is famous for its beautiful silk cloth. The Chinese discovered silkworms and perfected the skill of making silk about 4,000 years ago. Silk was manufactured and exported for a lot of money, and the Chinese tried to keep the secret of silk-making from foreign traders for hundreds of years. The ancient Romans once described Chinese embroidery on silk as 'painting with a needle', and spent huge amounts of money importing silk to Rome.

▲ This woman, wearing a traditional costume, is demonstrating how to weave cloth with silk threads.

Together with hemp, silk was the main material for clothing in China until around AD 500–700. Then, cotton imported from India became more common for most people to wear. Some people in rural areas wore clothing made from straw or bamboo, such as straw capes for rainy weather.

▶ At this bustling rural market, people are wearing a mixture of traditional clothing and Western-style dress.

Children's Clothes

▼ **This boy is wearing a red silk ceremonial costume. The flowers embroidered on the robe will bring him good luck.**

Children in China are traditionally dressed in bright colours when they are very young. Red and pink are especially lucky colours. Designs that show flowers and fruits, which symbolize long life for the Chinese, were once embroidered on silk or cotton clothes to bring the child a healthy life.

Hats in the shape of the faces of fierce animals were worn to scare away evil spirits, and shoes had animal faces with large eyes and ears to see and hear danger coming. Bells were attached to clothing to warn away bad spirits. Today, most children in China wear trainers, jeans and T-shirts.

Adults' Clothes

Traditional dress for adults is not as colourful as that for children. Men and women used to wear an overlapping short coat or jacket over trousers. For more formal occasions, men wore the coat over a long gown, while ladies wore a jacket over a long skirt, or sometimes trousers. Ladies in Hong Kong are famous for their *cheung sam*, a tight-fitting silk dress with a high neck, slit hem and knot buttons called 'frogs'. The *cheung sam* is still fashionable today.

▶ **This woman is wearing a simple cotton outfit for working in the fields.**

18

Wedding Clothes

Many Chinese brides wear a traditional long skirt and heavily embroidered jacket in red or black for part of their wedding day. They also wear a special head-dress made of gilded silver, with a red veil to hide the face, and a red sash over one shoulder. The sash would traditionally be used later as a baby carrier. Bridegrooms wear a blue or black long gown, with a small black hat.

▼ **This young couple have just got married. Red banners pinned to the door of their house wish them good luck.**

Embroider a good luck message to a friend. Find a small piece of red material – a handkerchief will do. Write your special message neatly on to the material in pen. Now, with some bright coloured thread, carefully sew over your writing. If you are good at sewing, you might like to add some lucky flowers or fruit to the design.

▶ A bride and groom pose for their wedding photographs.

At some Hong Kong weddings, the guests sign their names and good-luck messages on to a red silk banner with an embroidered dragon or phoenix design. Later, the banner may be sent to someone to embroider over the signatures as a keepsake. The dragon and the phoenix are traditional symbols of the emperor and empress, meaning that the newlyweds are 'royal' for the day.

MUSIC AND DANCE

Bells and chimes have been central to Chinese music since ancient times. Large sets of bell chimes, with up to sixty bells in various sizes, have been found in 3,000-year-old tombs. Bells and chimes are still a feature of modern Chinese music. Other popular instruments include the *hu qin*, a two-stringed instrument played with a bow, the *pipa*, a type of lute plucked like a guitar, and two kinds of flute, the *xiao* and the *sheng*.

Musicians, dancers, singers, storytellers, puppeteers and acrobats are all popular entertainers in China today. Chinese acrobats have been amazing their audiences for 2,000 years with stunts such as balancing another person on their head while standing on a stack of ten chairs!

▶ Chinese acrobats regularly amaze their audiences in shows all over the world.

▼ Folk dancers perform an energetic dance in traditional costume.

22

Dragon and Lion Dancers

Young men perform lion and dragon dances on special occasions, such as Chinese New Year. The costumes have large, papier-mâché heads, and cloth bodies which are carried by up to twelve dancers, depending on the length of the dragon's or lion's body.

▼ **The dragon dance was originally a folk dance to pray for rain, since the dragon is associated with water.**

Dragon and lion dances are very exciting to watch. The dancers use a lot of energy to move the head and body through the streets in bold movements.

Lion dances are divided into two groups – 'gentle' and 'military'. But there are also 'fire' lion dances and 'velvet' lion dances. These dances are usually performed as part of an acrobatic show.

Music on the Move

Over 1,000 years ago, court music from ancient China found its way to Japan. This tradition died out in China, but classical orchestras in Japan still play this music. Recent changes in China have meant that many different kinds of music are now popular, including Chinese pop music and rock and roll.

▶ **This young musician is playing a traditional flute.**

Chinese Opera

Opera began in China about 900 years ago. The stories are usually based on legends or historical events, involving characters such as brave heroes, kidnapped princesses and wicked emperors.

▼ **This performer at the Beijing Opera is dressed as a beautiful princess. Traditionally, female characters were always played by men.**

Design your own opera mask. Using coloured paper and paints you can create the face of a wicked villain, a brave hero or a beautiful princess. When you have finished your design, ask an adult to carefully copy it on to your face, using water-based face paints.

▲ **An opera performer puts on some make-up before a show.**

Opera performers dance and sing in an old style of Chinese language that not many people can understand today. The singers wear elaborate costumes and make-up, and use gestures and body movements to help the audience understand what is happening on stage. Colours are important symbols in Chinese opera – a red costume represents a loyal person, a black costume a bold person, and a white costume an evil person. The make-up designs also tell the audience more about the characters.

Chinese opera companies travel to many countries, giving performances to audiences around the world. Opera performances long ago sometimes took up to three days, but now they are only about three hours long.

RELIGION AND FESTIVALS

China has no official religion, but there are many folk beliefs and traditions in Chinese life. Two philosophies, Confucianism and Daoism, also influence the Chinese. Folk religion is based on ancient myths and legends about gods, demons and spirits. Many tales of gods are set in the mountains, where legend says that the Immortals, superior beings that knew the secret of eternal life, were found.

Confucius lived over 2,000 years ago. He said that people should behave in an honest, courageous, polite and correct way. Chinese people still follow Confucian ideas of how to behave.

▼ **Outside a temple, people burn offerings of incense and paper so that the smoke rises up to heaven, taking their wishes with it.**

▲ These Tibetans are sticking lucky money to a temple bell. They hope the bell's chimes will carry their wishes for luck and wealth to their ancestors.

Daoism is based on the writing of Lao Zi, who lived around the same time as Confucius. He wrote about *yin* and *yang*, the two opposite forces that the Chinese believe make up the universe. *Yin* is feminine, soft, left and cool, while *Yang* is masculine, hard, right and warm. Chinese people today try to keep a balance between *yin* and *yang* in their lives.

World Religions

Buddhism came to China as early as the first century BC. It was introduced by traders from India. There, Buddhism had grown out of the teachings of Prince Siddharta, who gave up his life of luxury to seek enlightenment. Buddhists follow his teachings, which say that people are reborn many times, and each time their situation depends on their behaviour in the previous life. In order to deserve a good life, you must live a good life. But a wicked person will have a life of misery and suffering when they are reborn. Buddhists believe that they can be reborn as people, animals, or even insects.

There are a small number of Muslims and Christians in China. Muslims live mainly in the western regions of China. They follow the religion of Islam, founded in Arabia during the seventh century, and brought to China by traders. Christianity was first brought to China by European missionaries during the sixteenth century.

▼ **These Tibetan monks have shaved their heads as a sign that they have given up their vanity and their worldly goods.**

▲ These Muslims in Lanzhou kneel to pray five times each day. They have taken their shoes off as a mark of respect.

Saying prayers and giving food offerings to ancestors is an important part of Chinese family life. People believe that if they take care of the needs of their family members in the next world, they in turn will bring good luck to the living family.

Happy New Year!

Chinese New Year is the most important Chinese festival. It falls between late January and early February. The week before New Year, people clean their houses from top to bottom and burn paper models of the Kitchen God and the God of Wealth. Chinese families believe that this is the way to send news to Heaven about how well the family has done during the year. Special red envelopes filled with money are given to children, and families pay special respect to their ancestors at this time.

▼ *Ching Ming* is the day when people visit family tombs to pay their respects. It is traditional to eat a picnic with their departed family.

32

▲ **Lion dancers celebrate the Chinese New Year while firecrackers are set off.**

In China, each year is named after one of the twelve animals of the traditional zodiac. A legend says that twelve animals came to visit the Buddha when he asked for visitors. As a reward, the Buddha named the years after each animal as they came before him. The Chinese believe that people take on the special qualities of the animal of their birth year, for instance the cleverness of a monkey, or the patience of an ox. The twelve animals are the rat, ox, tiger, rabbit, dragon, snake, horse, ram, monkey, rooster, pig and dog.

Other Celebrations

The Dragon Boat Festival welcomes the beginning of summer. The festival marks the death of a wise official who threw himself into a lake to protest at the actions of a wicked emperor. To keep his body from being eaten by dragons and wicked demons, the people of the village raced in boats to protect him by tempting the demons with sweet rice dumplings. Today, in Hong Kong, clubs and organizations race in colourful boats to remind themselves of this event.

▼ **These people are preparing their boat for a race in the Dragon Boat Festival in Hong Kong.**

34

▲ These children have lit candles for the Moon Festival.

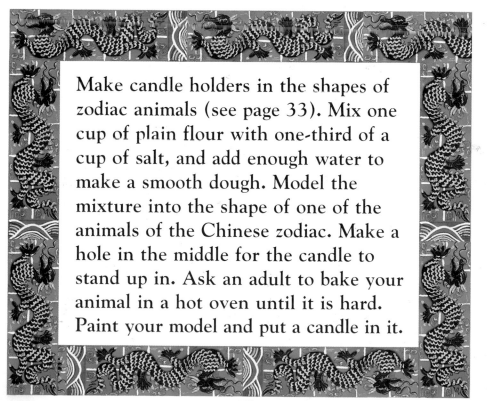

Make candle holders in the shapes of zodiac animals (see page 33). Mix one cup of plain flour with one-third of a cup of salt, and add enough water to make a smooth dough. Model the mixture into the shape of one of the animals of the Chinese zodiac. Make a hole in the middle for the candle to stand up in. Ask an adult to bake your animal in a hot oven until it is hard. Paint your model and put a candle in it.

The Moon Festival is held in early autumn to give thanks for a successful harvest. People go out at night, carrying paper lanterns in the shape of fish or birds. Children try to see the Rabbit and the Three-legged Toad who live on the moon, according to traditional folk stories. People exchange sweet moon cakes, filled with red bean curd, almond paste, or egg.

CHINA AT PLAY

Many traditional games and sports for adults and children grew out of skills that were practised by warriors and soldiers in ancient China. Kite-flying, archery, wrestling and horse riding were very popular. Other games, such as complicated board games, were part of the amusements at the royal palaces.

Some of these traditional sports, such as martial arts, are now practised and studied all over the world. Judo is now an Olympic sport. *Tai ji*, a Daoist form of exercise, is now very popular in the West. *Tai ji* requires great concentration to keep the body in constant movement, without losing balance.

▼ **A group of children practise their basketball skills. Basketball is becoming a popular sport in China.**

▲ **This boy is having fun on a swing in a local park.**

'Small games' is what Chinese people call keeping little pets, such as songbirds, pigeons, and even crickets. Ladies of the Imperial Court kept crickets in golden cages, but people today keep their crickets in cages made from bamboo. Crickets are easy to feed, and they 'sing' as well.

Kite Flying

Kites were originally invented in China to send messages back and forth between different groups of the ancient emperors' armies during battle. Today, they are enjoyed by people all over the world. In the Far East and South-east Asia, kite-flying is popular with adults as well as children. Many boys and girls of all ages in almost every country now know about and fly kites. Special kites, such as 'fighting kites' or 'singing kites', are very popular.

▼ **A boy takes his small kite for a test flight.**

Why not make your own kite? Draw your design on a large piece of paper. Popular Chinese designs are butterflies, birds and dragons. Colour the design in brightly. Tape two lightweight sticks together to make a cross shape, and stick the paper design to the frame. Tie a string to the frame. If you make your kite big enough and light enough it will fly!

Keeping Fit

City people use parks or community centres called 'Cultural Palaces' for sport. They play all kinds of sports such as Ping-Pong, which might be considered China's national sport, basketball, volleyball, swimming and shadow boxing. Ping-Pong is played indoors in winter, but in summer, people play almost anywhere, in parks, school playgrounds and quiet streets. Rural Chinese people don't have as many facilities as those living in the cities, but board games, such as chess and draughts, are popular.

▼ **The Chinese believe that exercise is very important. These people are keeping fit with some early morning disco exercises by the Yellow River.**

Card and Board Games

People in China play chess, but it is not the same as international chess. Although it involves 'taking' pieces from the other player, there are no pawns or knights, and no queen or king. Chinese chess is played with flat, black and white stones on a grid board. This game is very popular in Japan, and is known there and abroad as 'Go'.

Mah Jong is a popular game in China played with ivory tiles. The tiles make a loud clicking noise as the players move them quickly around the table.

▼ **Playing cards were invented in China. These traditional playing cards are made from wood.**

Other Games

Chinese children play *ti jian zi*, a game of skill in which a person tries to keep a small ball in the air, using only their ankles, knees, and thighs. They are not allowed to use their hands. 'Kick the Bag' is another version of this, and can be played by one or more children in a circle, where the bag must be kept moving for the whole game. Children also play a game called 'Five Stones' which is similar to Jacks.

▲ **Chinese chess is one of the oldest games in the world and was invented over 4,000 years ago. It is still popular.**

STORY TIME

In ancient China, musicians played and dancers danced while
storytellers sang their stories and poems. People learned how
to write poetry as an important part of their education.
Actors, singers, puppets, and now films and television retell
old stories and favourite poems along with new ones to delight
people of all ages. Perhaps the most famous story in eastern
Asia is that of the Monkey King, who journeyed to the West
to find the secret of enlightenment and immortality.
This story was originally written in the
sixteenth century in several parts.

The Monkey King and his Journey to the West

In the far away Mountain of Flowers and Fruit, a very unusual stone began to change and grow into an egg shape. The light of the sun and the moon, and the blessings of heaven and earth helped it to change. Suddenly it hatched and out jumped a stone monkey.

Monkey was soon jumping about and playing with other lively monkeys. One day, whilst playing, they came to a raging waterfall, and they gathered around, chattering and crying.

'Silly monkeys,' Monkey said. 'I'm not afraid of a little waterfall. Follow me!' And he leaped right into the waterfall and out the other side. All the other monkeys followed him into the white, foamy water. The monkeys were so grateful to come out safely, that they made Monkey their Great King. But soon, the Monkey King became very sad.

'What is making you feel so sad, Your Majesty?' asked the other monkeys.

'I am thinking how unfair it is that I will grow old one day and finally die. How much better if I could live for ever! I must search for the land of the Immortals for, like buddhas and holy sages, they never die. I am the greatest monkey in the universe, and I should be an Immortal and live in the Paradise of the Western Mountains.' And so he decided to search for the secrets of the Immortals.

Monkey travelled for a long time, over rivers and oceans, over plains and mountains. Finally, a friendly woodcutter told him how to find the Cave of the Moon and the Three Stars, where the Immortal teacher, Master Subodhi, lived with his students. Monkey hurried to Master Subodhi's cave.

'Master, I have come a long way to find you. Now, tell me quickly the secret of Immortality!' said Monkey.

The Monkey King

'Not so fast, you bold monkey!' said Master Subodhi. 'First you must work and study like the other students here.' In spite of his rude behaviour, Monkey was accepted as a student. Every day there were lessons in being polite, studying and asking questions correctly, and in languages, holy books, and handwriting. In between lessons, Monkey worked in the gardens, sweeping and digging, planting and pruning. He also had to gather firewood, bring water from the well, and take cool drinks and tea to Master Subodhi and the other students.

In this way, several years passed, and although Monkey was always in and out of trouble, one day the Master finally told him the secret of Immortality. Monkey learned how to fly, and could walk over the clouds. Then, he learned how to change himself into other shapes. Monkey was still very naughty, and he could not resist bragging and showing off his powers to other students. But the secret of Immortality was only for those who had also learned lessons of wisdom, humility and kindness. Master Subodhi decided to send Monkey away, in disgrace.

But Monkey could not stay out of trouble for long. He was never satisfied, and went on adventures to distant lands. Searching for more powers, he managed to create such a commotion with the Dragon Kings of the Four Oceans, that he was called to visit the Celestial Jade Emperor. The Emporer had received many complaints about the naughty immortal monkey.

'Excellent!' said Monkey. 'I have been wanting to take a little trip to Heaven… this is perfect!' He had no idea of the real reason for the Jade Emperor's message.

The Jade Emperor decided to pardon Monkey for his bad behaviour, but kept him in Heaven so that he could be watched, and so that he could learn to behave himself. Monkey was commanded to take charge of the heavenly stable, with 1,000 heavenly horses in his care. Naturally, Monkey could not keep out of mischief, and was transferred to take care of the Garden of Immortal Peaches.

The Monkey King

But even here, Monkey managed to misbehave. When the Jade Empress called for her Immortal Peaches to be gathered for a banquet, she discovered that Monkey had not only eaten most of them, but was sleeping in a peach tree when he should have been working! Finally, the Jade Emperor had to punish Monkey, and he sent his soldiers to capture Monkey in a fierce battle. With the Buddha's help, Monkey was captured, and put into a crack in the mountain to stay until he learned to be good.

After 500 years, two travellers on their way to the capital city released Monkey. The three friends went on together. In the capital they met Hsuan-tsang, a monk chosen by the T'ang Emperor to go to India to search for the Holy Books of Buddhism, which were called the Tripitaka. The Emperor ordered Hsuan-tsang to change his name to Tripitaka too, to mark the importance of the journey.

Tripitaka, Monkey, and their two companions set out on their long journey to India. Along the way, they found many adventures, and each new difficulty taught them something new as they searched for the Holy Books. Finally they came to the land of the Flaming Mountain, which stood right in the way of the road to the West. In order to pass the mountain, Monkey, Tripitaka and the others had to conquer two ferocious demons – Rakshasi and her husband, Bull Demon King. That was not easy, but after several frightful battles, when heads flew, and magic curses shot back and forth, Monkey and his friends continued their journey to the West.

Tired, but calm and peaceful, Monkey and the others travelled on, until at last they came to the great monastery where the sacred books were kept. Here, the Lord Buddha sat on his lotus throne surrounded by his attendants and saints. Monkey, Tripitaka and the others bowed down to him, and told him of their search, to take the words of the Buddha back to China. The Buddha granted this wish, and sent the travellers back to China in a magical wind. There they were welcomed, and even the naughty Monkey became a hero!

TOPIC WEB

HISTORY
- Imperial China
- Social customs

R.E.
- Festivals
- Role of music
- Role of clothing
- Buddhism
- Christianity
- Islam

SCIENCE
- Vibration and sound
- Nutritional value of food

DESIGN AND TECHNOLOGY
- Design a kite
- Design a mask
- Clothes for different temperatures

GEOGRAPHY
- Clothes and their purpose
- Types of weather and their advantages and disadvantages
- Types of food grown in different countries
- Farming

TRADITIONS FROM CHINA

ENGLISH
- Library skills
- Creative writing
- Myths
- Signs and symbols

P.E./DANCE/DRAMA
- Creating characters through dance

MUSIC
- Exploring rhythm
- Making sounds
- Percussion instruments

MATHS
- Patterns drawn from Chinese traditions

ART AND CRAFT
- Mixing colours
- Embroidery
- Weaving
- Face painting
- Patterns and textures of materials

GLOSSARY

Ancestors Family members who have died.

Bamboo A type of woody grass which is hollow and is sometimes used to make furniture.

Banquets Special dinners for a group of people.

Delta The place at the mouth of a river where it splits into several channels.

Ethnic minorities A small group of people whose racial or cultural background is different from the main population.

Exported Goods sold to another country.

Hemp A plant which has fibres that can be used to make rope and fabrics.

Host A person who holds a meal or a party for guests.

Lute A string instrument, like a guitar, with a long neck and a pear-shaped body.

Martial arts Fighting sports such as judo and karate.

Meditation Deep and continued thought.

Missionaries People who go abroad to do religious work.

Opera A play in which the words are sung.

Philosophies Ideas about human behaviour.

Provinces Large areas and divisions of a country.

Puppeteers People who work puppets.

Sub-tropical A region next to or bordering a tropical area.

Staple foods The important or main parts of people's everyday diet.

Trade routes Routes used by people travelling from one area to another, to buy and sell goods.

Zodiac A large, imaginary belt in the heavens, divided into twelve sections. Each section of the Chinese zodiac is named after an animal.

FURTHER INFORMATION

Non-fiction:
A Family From China by Julia Waterlow (Wayland, 1998)

C is for China by Sungwan So (Francis Lincoln, 1997)

China (Country Insights series) by Julia Waterlow (Wayland, 1996)

Traditions Around the World series (Wayland, 1995)

World Religions by John Barker (Dorling Kindersley, 1997)

Fiction:
Chinese Myths and Legends retold by Philip Ardagh (Belitha Press, 1996)

The Emperor and the Nightingale by Meilo So (Francis Lincoln, 1997)

Useful Addresses:
British Museum, Great Russell Street, London WC1B 3DG Tel: 0207 323 8299.

Cultural Section, Chinese Embassy, 11 West Heath Road, London NW3 Tel: 0207 631 1430.

The Great Britain–China Centre, 15 Belgrave Square, London SW1X 8PS Tel: 0207 235 6696.

INDEX

Page numbers in **bold** refer to photographs.